NEVER
— *say* —
NEVER

The Peter Principle

A Topical Bible Study Workbook
for Women

by
Catherine G. Swift

ISBN 1-58427-136-1

Guardian of Truth Foundation
P.O. Box 9670
Bowling Green, Kentucky 42102

Special thanks to the precious women who have encouraged me in the writing and publishing of these lessons. Also to those who have taught me so much while attending the "Never say NEVER" classes.

GOD BLESS YOU!

Contents

Introduction 1

Lesson 1   "God forbid...this should NEVER happen."
On Commitment 7

Lesson 2   "...NEVER shall you wash my feet!"
On Service versus Pride 17

Lesson 3   "I will NEVER fall away."
On Taking a Stand 27

Lesson 4   "I have NEVER eaten anything unholy or unclean..."
On Prejudice 37

Lesson 5   "...I have NEVER been eloquent..."
On Teaching 47

Lesson 6   "I shall NEVER be moved."
On Marital Fidelity 57

Lesson 7   "I will NEVER forgive him for that."
On Forgiveness 67

Lesson 8   "My children will NEVER do that."
On Parenting 79

Lesson 9   "I NEVER said I was perfect."
On Being Complete 91

Lesson 10   "You will NEVER amount to anything."
On Encouraging 101

Lesson 11   "Me submit ? ....NEVER!"
On Humility 111

Lesson 12   "I could NEVER cope with that."
On Suffering 121

Lesson 13   Only God can say "NEVER."
On God's Promises 131

Notes to the Teacher 141

Introduction

Introduction

Have you ever said "I'll NEVER"…do this or that…only to find yourself, at a later date, doing that very thing? It's a good thing the Lord didn't put calories into words, isn't it? I for one would certainly be obese from eating so many of mine!

Is this an uncommon problem? I don't think so, since we find any number of times in the scriptures where someone has had to struggle with it. Of course, the one who comes most readily to our mind is the apostle Peter. On several occasions he would say "NEVER"…only to regret the word. That is why we call this caution to never say "NEVER" the Peter Principle.

However, we will see that Peter was definitely not the only one who had the problem. In fact, I rather think that Adam and Eve, in all their innocence, while in the garden surely thought, if not declared, that they would NEVER disobey God. Why, He had given them life and each other. He walked and talked with them and enjoyed a close relationship with them. When the serpent confronted Eve, to entice her, she repeated to him just what God had instructed them.

> *And the woman said to the serpent, "From the fruit of the trees of the garden we may eat; but from the fruit of the tree which is in the middle of the garden God has said, 'you shall not eat from it or touch it, lest you die!'"*
> —Genesis 3:2, 3

But there is something about the moment that comes…and it does come…that changes everything, at least in our mind. Eve began to "see" things from a different perspective. She entertained a new point of view. This fruit looked good! In fact, it looked delicious and not only that, it would make her wise. Well now, that makes a difference, doesn't it? God would want them to enjoy this yummy, all natural fruit, wouldn't He? He would surely want them to be wise, wouldn't He?

It is so easy to get carried away, isn't it? But once the deed is done…you know, the one we would "NEVER" do…then come the consequences; and they will come!

In Adam and Eve's lives the most important relationship they had, or could have, was shattered and there was no way to undo what they had done. Their innocence was gone!

> *Then the Lord God said, "Behold, the man has become like one of us, knowing good and evil; and now, lest he stretch out his hand, and take from the tree of life and eat, and live forever"…*
> *Therefore the Lord God sent him out of the garden of Eden, to cultivate the ground from which he was taken. So He drove the man out; and at the east of the garden of Eden He stationed the cherubim, and the flaming sword which turned every direction, to guard the way to the tree of life.*
>
> —Genesis 3:22–24

But there are many facets of The Peter Principle. There are not only those things we will "NEVER" do that we shouldn't, there are things we think we can "NEVER" do that we should and those we are sure should "NEVER" happen that should. Peter, just as you and I, had trouble with all of them. We will find other bible characters did too. Often the attitude is present even if the "NEVER" isn't stated.

There is an old adage that states "to be forewarned is to be forearmed." I have found from my own experience that when I am prepared for the worst, it seldom happens. That is the reason for these lessons; that we might examine some of the areas where this Peter Principle sneaks up on us and try to be forearmed and prepared. Hopefully, we will be able to avoid some of the heartache that comes from saying "NEVER."

"Therefore, let him who thinks he stands take heed lest he fall."

— 1 Corinthians 10:12

Lesson 1

"God forbid. . . this should NEVER happen."

On Commitment

On Commitment

READ: Matthew 16:13–23

Parallel accounts: Mark 8:27–37; Luke 9:18–23

Isn't life full of peaks and valleys? This passage and others we will be looking at really show the contrast. Just when we think we are making some progress...we embarrass ourselves! Perhaps that is why it is so easy for most of us to identify with Peter.

In the context Peter has just shown his understanding of who Jesus was. Jesus has said that Peter's confession will be the very foundation of His church. In fact, Peter will have the privilege of opening the way, which is seen in Acts 2 when he preaches the gospel on the day of Pentecost. How special Peter must have felt. What a high point in his life!

However, the "peaks" are slippery and we don't seem to stay there very long. Jesus began to show His disciples the things He would have to suffer and Peter "rebuked Him." Can you imagine rebuking the Son of God? "God forbid, Lord, this shall NEVER happen to you."

Jesus called Peter "Satan." Explain why. Compare Matthew 4:1–11.

What would the outcome have been if Peter (Satan) had had his way?

What was Peter's problem?

Did anyone else ever have this problem? Do we? See Philippians 2:19–21; 3:18, 19.

In Matthew 16:24–28, Jesus teaches Peter and the others how to overcome this problem with commitment. Note what this involves.

What seems to be the problem these people were having with commitment?

What do the following passages tell us about a life that is committed to God?

Romans 6:1–11

On Commitment

Romans 12:1, 2

2 Corinthians 5:17

Galatians 3:27

Ephesians 4:22–25

Colossians 3:1–11

Read Philippians 2:5–8 and note the elements of Jesus' attitude toward commitment.

The proper attitude of commitment gives us respect for authority. Jesus is, as always, our prime example. Matthew 3:13–15; 26:36–46. What was the basic element of His prayer?

What is my personal attitude in this area? Have I made a complete commitment?

What basic problem must we overcome?

It would be nice if we could point to a passage following Peter's rebuke of Jesus that would show he quickly learned and practiced the essence of commitment. But alas, Peter was like most of us; it took him awhile. Perhaps his next "NEVER" statement and it's consequences made it all a little clearer to him.

On Commitment

Notes

Lesson 2

". . . NEVER shall you wash my feet!"

On Service versus Pride

On Service versus Pride

READ: Luke 22:7–16; 24–30; John 13:1–20

These passages, as well as other gospel accounts, show us the intimate gathering of Jesus' closest companions the night before His death. We also see the startling contrast in attitudes. Some time earlier in the evening the twelve had a dispute over which one of them was regarded to be greatest. Jesus gives them credit for standing by Him but adds that they must learn to serve.

A little later He puts on a surprise demonstration as He takes a basin of water and a towel and begins to wash their feet. There is no record of any comments from any of the other men until He comes to Peter, who seems dismayed. "Lord, do you wash my feet?" Even though Jesus assures him he will understand later, Peter can't allow it... "NEVER shall you wash my feet!"

Peter had just observed Jesus washing the feet of the others. Why do you think he thought the Lord should not wash his?

Jesus answered ..."If I do not wash you, you have no part with me!" Explain why.

What is indicated by Peter's reply..."Then wash my whole body..."?

He certainly wanted

Read Matthew 20:25–28. Even though this was a specific lesson for the apostles, what can we learn from it?

What happened in the early church when this lesson was forgotten? See Acts 20:17, 28–29; 3 John 9–11.

Can you think of a radical example that exists in the religious world today?

Consider these passages:

Psalm 138:6

Proverbs 11:2

Proverbs 16:5

Proverbs 18:12

Proverbs 25:27

Proverbs 29:23

Acts 10:23–26

What is it we can take pride in? See Jeremiah 9:23, Galatians 6:14.

On Service versus Pride

What do the following passages tell us about the Christian life?

Romans 7:6

Romans 12:1–2, 9–21

1 Corinthians 12:25–27

Galatians 5:13

Ephesians 4:11–13

Philippians 2:3–4

1 Peter 5:5–7

According to Hebrews 12:28–29, what should motivate us to serve? Add other passages that express why we should serve God and others.

How important is an attitude of willing service? See Matthew 25:31–46 and Colossians 3:23.

We have looked at pride versus service and know that Peter must have gained something from Jesus' demonstration. But like any other principle...it is one thing in theory and another in practice. Next we find Peter getting still another lesson in the "nitty gritty" of life in Christ.

On Service versus Pride

Notes

Lesson 3

"I will NEVER fall away."

On Taking a Stand

On Taking a Stand

READ: Matthew 26:20–35

Picture what you have just read. These men had spent the evening celebrating a memorial meal of great meaning to them as Jews. This meal was to be eaten with family as they remembered how God had delivered their forefathers from Egyptian slavery. This was a close knit group.

Some were actually siblings, fleshly brothers: Peter and Andrew, James and John. For several years they had spent much of their time following and listening to this teacher, Jesus. They had watched as He healed the sick, raised the dead, and defied nature in other amazing ways. He had even given them the power to do some of the same things. They had come to recognize Him as the promised Messiah. He was the "man of the hour" and they were His best friends!

He had told them earlier that one of them was going to betray Him. How could this be? They were confused. As they walked to the Mount of Olives, Jesus realized they still did not understand the things He had been trying to tell them; that He would suffer and die, then be resurrected. He tried again by telling them they would all "fall away." Here Peter made his declaration.

> *"Even though all may fall away because of you, I will NEVER fall away."*

What does it mean to "fall away"?

Was Peter the only one who had a "NEVER" response? verse 35

What did Jesus say would be the cause of their "falling"?

On Taking a Stand

Read Matthew 26:69–75; Luke 22:54–62; John 18:25–27. How did Peter "fall away"? Be specific.

Read Matthew 27:1–5; 2 Corinthians 7:9, 10; Hebrews 6:4–6. Contrast the "falling" of Peter with that of Judas.

PETER	JUDAS

Consider the parable of the "talents." Matthew 25:14–30. Thinking of each "talent" as an opportunity, how would it relate to this chapter?

What is the alternative to denying Jesus?

Thinking about Peter's declaration in this chapter, what are some ways that we might "fall away" or deny the Lord?

What might be the cause of our stumbling?

How might we prepare ourselves for these times so that we may not fall?

What if we realize that we have failed to take a stand for Jesus when we had the opportunity? What should we do?

Can you think of a scripture passage that would help either before or after?

Notes

Lesson 4

"I have NEVER eaten anything
unholy or unclean. . ."

On Prejudice

Lesson 4   "I have NEVER eaten anything unholy or unclean..."

On Prejudice

READ: Acts 10:1–34

Peter, as a Jew, grew up with a strict dietary code. This can be reviewed in Leviticus 11 and Deuteronomy 14. However, the vision the Lord showed Peter in this account and the lesson he must learn from it weren't about food. This was about people!

We have considered how pride works against our life of service. Now let's think about prejudice and how it can creep in and catch us unaware.

When the Lord commanded, in the vision, "Arise, Peter, kill and eat," Peter's first response was defensive..."By no means, Lord, for I have NEVER eaten anything unholy or unclean." These were not just things you didn't eat, but he called them "common" and "profane"...indicating how he detested them.

Define the following words:

PARTIALITY

PREFERENCE

PREJUDICE

What was the Lord's response to Peter's statement?

Why do you think the vision was displayed three times? Does it tell us anything about our human willingness to accept change?

What did the relationship between Jews and Gentiles have to do with this?

What was the lesson that Peter said he now understood?

It is often difficult for us to appreciate the true hatred between Jews and Gentiles during this period. Yet we don't have to look far in our own history to find similar animosity. Though much has taken place in the way of change in the last forty years, there is still a great deal of prejudice among the races of people on the earth. But there are other areas in which we find prejudice.

List areas of prejudice that come to your mind.

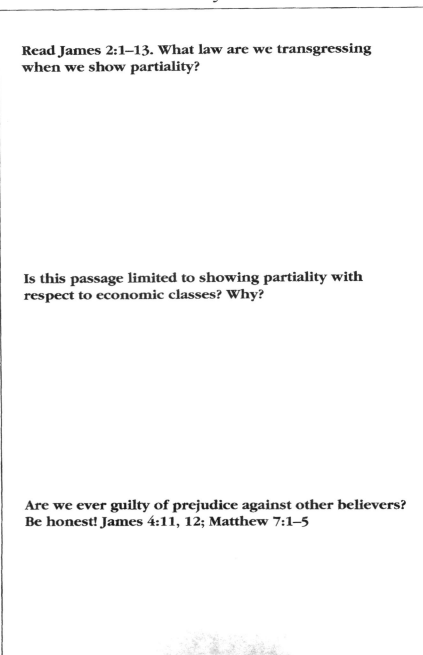

On Prejudice

Read James 2:1–13. What law are we transgressing when we show partiality?

Is this passage limited to showing partiality with respect to economic classes? Why?

Are we ever guilty of prejudice against other believers? Be honest! James 4:11, 12; Matthew 7:1–5

What did Jesus mean when He said, "Do not give what is holy to dogs and do not throw pearls before swine"? Matthew 7:6

Read and consider the following passages:

Proverbs 28:21

Matthew 22:15–17

Acts 10:34, 35

Romans 2:9–11

What can we do now to prevent ourselves from becoming prejudiced? How can we help our children avoid it?

How did Jesus say that we would be known as His disciples? See John 13:35.

How are Jesus' statements in Matthew 5:13–16 relative to this subject?

Notes

Lesson 5

"...I have NEVER been eloquent..."

On Teaching

On Teaching

READ: Exodus 3:7–12; 4:10–13; Acts 7:20–34. If you have never read the Old Testament, read Exodus 1–4.

Isn't it interesting that when we don't want to do something, we can always think of a "good" reason why we can't? Moses was no different than we are in that respect.

The conversation between Moses and God recorded in Exodus 3 and 4 almost sounds like a child arguing with his parent when given some chore to do. My paraphrase: "Why do I have to do this? (Ch. 3:11); "What shall I say?" (Ch. 3:13); "What if they won't believe me?" (Ch. 4:1); "But I'm not much of a talker" (Ch. 4:10); "Please send someone else" (Ch. 4:13). You can almost hear the whine in his voice.

Is it any wonder that God became angry with Moses? Exodus 4:14–16 tells us how God finally proposed to get the job done, but notice that Moses was not "off the hook"; he still had to tell Aaron what to say. Even though God would allow Aaron to be Moses' "mouth," Moses had to communicate with God. Though he claimed to be unskilled in speech, Moses always seemed to be able to talk to God, boldly. What meaning does this have for us?

What excuses do we use not to teach?

Read Romans 12:6–8; 1 Corinthians 12:28, 29; Ephesians 4:11. What impression do you get about teaching from these passages?

Is eloquence of the most importance when it comes to teaching God's word? Acts 18:24–26; 1 Corinthians 1:17; 2 Corinthians 11:16

Certainly we recognize that public speaking is one way to teach God's word, but is it really the most important way? How was the "good news" of Jesus spread so effectively in the early years after His resurrection? Acts 8:4

What is James saying in this passage? James 3:1

What did David say would motivate him to teach? Psalm 51:12, 13

To what extent are we all expected to "teach"? 1 Peter 3:1, 2; 14–16 Are we ever not teaching? Explain your answer.

In Titus 2:1–8, the evangelist is instructed to teach the people. Read this chapter a couple of times. Make note of each group and what they are to be taught. Then consider what other teaching will be done.

On Teaching

As women, what do you think our primary responsibility in teaching is?

What guidelines are suggested in these passages?

Deuteronomy 6:4–9

Proverbs 16:20–24

Proverbs 31:26

Romans 2:17–23

Note more guidelines from these passages:

Galatians 6:1

On Teaching

Ephesians 4:14–15

Colossians 3:16,17

Philippians 1:12–18

Philippians 2:1–3

What can we do now to be prepared for "teaching" opportunities?

We know from following the rest of Moses' life that he became not only an eloquent teacher but a powerful leader. He was able to do the job that God chose for him to do. We are no different, in that whatever place God has given us we are able to accomplish what He wants. (Philippians 4:13; Hebrews 13:6; 1 John 4:4)

Notes

Lesson 6

". . . I shall NEVER be moved."

On Marital Fidelity

On Marital Fidelity

READ: Psalm 30:6; 2 Samuel 11–12

Have you ever considered the fact that David was surprised when he realized Nathan's story of accusation was about him? Have you ever wondered how someone who loved God could commit adultery and plot murder?

We talked before of "peaks and valleys." David had certainly had a lot of "peaks." Singled out and favored by God, through Samuel, God's prophet. (1 Samuel 16:1–13) He was favored by King Saul. (1 Samuel 16:21, 22) A hero for slaying Goliath. (1 Samuel 17) Praised by the people. (1 Samuel 18:6, 7) King over Israel and Judah at age 30. (2 Samuel 5:3–5) Triumphant over his nation's enemies. (2 Samuel 8) It must have been during one of these prosperous times when David said to himself and to God "...I shall NEVER be moved!"

But then came a valley. Satan loves these times in our lives. Times when we are unsuspecting and vulnerable to temptation.

Consider 2 Samuel 11:1–4 and note the circumstances.

List the consequences of this one evening of pleasure.

Did there seem to be concern for the consequences at the time? In what way?

David was a man devoted to God, yet the time came in his life when his focus turned to what he wanted instead of what God wanted for him. All the right elements were present to set him up for a trial that tested him like never before.

Remember another man also devoted to God, all at once faced with a compromising situation? Read Genesis 39:1–20.

On Marital Fidelity

Having read both the account of David and of Joseph, what similarities are there? What differences? List them in two columns.

SIMILAR	DIFFERENT

Galatians 6:1 tells us to help someone "caught" in a trespass with a spirit of gentleness. Explain why.

On Marital Fidelity

Adultery is not a new problem. Using your concordance, find some passages that deal with this problem. List them and a short summary in your own words.

Social scientists tell us that all known cultures have some kind of law against extramarital sex relations and a mandatory punishment. Yet in our modern age marital infidelity is no longer called "sin" or considered disgraceful. It hardly produces guilt but is called an "affair." Unfortunately, it is no longer unheard of even in the church.

What are some things that are feeding the fire of this problem?

On Marital Fidelity

What are some of the elements that might allow Satan to set us up like he did David?

Have you ever considered yourself beyond temptation in this area?

What about fantasizing? See Matthew 5:28; James 1:14, 15.

Where does purity of action begin? Matthew 5:8; Titus 1:15

How can we prepare ourselves to have Joseph's reaction to temptation in this area, instead of David's?

Notes

Lesson 7

"I will NEVER forgive him for that."

On Forgiveness

On Forgiveness

READ: Genesis 27:1–46

> *"Esau bore a grudge against Jacob because of
> the blessing with which his father had blessed
> him; and Esau said to himself, 'the days of the
> mourning for my father are near; then I will
> kill my brother Jacob.'"*

Can you feel any empathy for Esau in these circumstances?
Have you ever been wronged by someone so ruthlessly? Have
you ever shared his feeling of frustration and said in your
heart…"I will NEVER forgive him/her for that"?

To suffer the pain of betrayal or the humiliation of ill treatment
and have the guilty party go on their merry way without any
visible consequences…seems there is no justice.

What about Joseph, the somewhat arrogant teenager who so
irritated his ten older brothers they threatened to kill him, but
finally sold him into slavery in a foreign land? Genesis 37:1–28

Though God blessed Joseph while he was in Egypt, he was
again unjustly treated, and because of false accusations spent
time in a prison. Wouldn't this produce bitterness and hatred
in the hearts of most of the people we know? What about
yourself? Would it be easy to have a forgiving spirit in these
kinds of situations?

Is a forgiving spirit a natural thing? How can we acquire it?
first let's consider just how important it is.

On Forgiveness

What did Jesus say is dependent on our willingness to forgive? Mark 11:25, 26; Matthew 6:14, 15

When Peter came to Jesus and asked how often he should forgive his brother, what do you think he was really looking for? Matthew 18:21, 22. Did he find it?

Read Luke 17:1–10. What is the meaning of verses 7–10? Consider the entire context.

On Forgiveness

What do these passages have to do with forgiveness?
John 13:33, 34

Colossians 3:14

1 John 3:7–12

1 Peter 3:8, 9

What is involved in forgiving "as God in Christ has forgiven you"? Ephesians 4:32

Now that we understand the importance of forgiveness how do we go about it? It isn't an easy process. Let's look at some examples that might help us. Read Genesis 32:3–6; 33:1–4; and 45:1–15.

This is first to encourage us! If Esau and Joseph could forgive the terrible things that were done to them, surely we can find a way to forgive others.

In the parable of the prodigal (Luke 15:11–32) look at the actions of the father. If we are to forgive as God forgives us, what can we learn from this parable? Consider the different aspects of his attitude. Note what you find.

Read the letter of Philemon (in the Living Bible if you can). What is the apostle Paul asking Philemon to do?

On Forgiveness

**Read the following passages in the Philippian letter.
What do you think was a problem with these
Christians? Philippians 1:9, 27; 2:1–8, 12–16; 4:1–9**

**Read the following passages and note what they teach
us about our relationships.**

1 John 1:8–10

Matthew 5:21, 22

1 Corinthians 13:4–7

2 Corinthians 2:5–11

Ephesians 4:26, 27

James 1:19, 20

James 4:1–12

What is your definition of FORGIVENESS?

What kinds of things are hardest for you to forgive?

Is it possible to forgive someone who has not asked for your forgiveness? See Luke 23:34; Acts 7:59, 60; Romans 5:8.

What if you are the offender? What should your action be? Matthew 5:23, 24; Mark 9:43–50

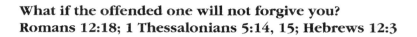

**What if the offended one will not forgive you?
Romans 12:18; 1 Thessalonians 5:14, 15; Hebrews 12:3**

**One·of the things that should help us keep a forgiving
attitude is to be keenly aware of our own need for
God's forgiveness. Romans 3:10, 23; James 3:2**

On Forgiveness

Notes

Lesson 8

"My children will NEVER *do that."*

On Parenting

On Parenting

READ: 1 Samuel 2:12–17, 22–25; 8:1–3.

How many parents do you suppose have choked on this phrase…"My children will NEVER do that!"

Samuel, as we learned in the early chapter of 1 Samuel, was raised from the time he was weaned, by Eli the priest. He had been used by God to predict the judgment of Eli's house because of the sins of his sons. 1 Samuel 3:11–18

Samuel had ample opportunity to see the consequences of unruly children. It is hard for me to imagine that he was so different from every other parent I have known (including myself) that he didn't at some point think to himself…"My children will NEVER do that." Yet here it is recorded in the pages of scripture…"his sons did not walk in his ways."

Why is it that people who love God and strive to serve Him sometimes have children who do not choose to do so? I do not have all the answers to that question. However, the bible gives us some ideas. Certainly God in His infinite wisdom saw fit to give man a will of his own, and ultimately we are each responsible for the consequences of our own choices.
2 Chronicles 25:4

Nevertheless, any right thinking parent wants to guide their child in the best way. Proverbs 22:6 What does the bible say that "way" is? Ephesians 6:4

Find as many translations as you can to compare the above passage. Look up definitions and give synonyms as you list each positive and each negative mentioned.

Positives	Negatives	Definitions & Synonyms

Read Hebrews 12:5–11 and Ephesians 6:4. Note the Greek word (*paideuo*) is translated both "discipline" and "admonish." Would you consider this a positive or negative aspect of training a child? Why?

What are the goals you want your training to accomplish? List them here.

Read Matthew 22:37–40; Ephesians 6:1–3. Can you make a comparison of these two passages?

Even if we taught our children perfectly, what is most likely to undo it, in your opinion?

What were Eli's weaknesses as a parent? 1 Samuel 2:27–31; 3:11–13

How might we exhibit the same attitude? Be specific.

What kind of father was Job? Job 1:2–8 In what ways can we follow his example?

Can you think of other bible examples of parents and the kind of influence they had on their children? What can we learn from them?

On Parenting

Read the following passages and note the elements of a parent's responsibility to their child. Can you add others?

Deuteronomy 6:4–9

Deuteronomy 21:18–21

Proverbs 23:13, 14

2 Corinthians 12:14

Ephesians 6:4

1 Timothy 5:8

Ask yourself these questions:

Which do you think of most often...the things you can do as a Christian or the things you can't do? How do you suppose this influences your child's thinking?

What do you consider to be the strongest anti-Christian influence in your life and that of your children? What can you do to change that?

Where do you honestly think their strongest Christian influence comes from? Where should it come from?

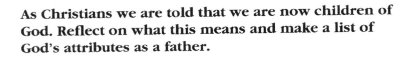

As Christians we are told that we are now children of God. Reflect on what this means and make a list of God's attributes as a father.

How can considering God's example be an encouragement and comfort to us as parents?

Notes

Lesson 9

"I NEVER *said I was perfect.*"

On Being Complete

On Being Complete

Some may not be able to relate to this "NEVER" statement at all. Yet others know quite well the frustration behind it. It is generally said to someone in self-defense, following criticism, or muttered under your breath when you haven't quite reached your own high standards.

The struggle with perfectionism is painful! If we can understand it better perhaps we can avoid passing it on to our children and be more complete ourselves.

Define PERFECTIONISM.

Let's look at some bible characters who may have had a little problem with this. Contrast the people in each story and see if you can show whether their focus is outward or inward.

Luke 10:38–42   Martha   Mary

On Being Complete

Luke 15:25–32   **Prodigal**   **Brother**

Luke 18:10–13   **Pharisee**   **Tax Gatherer**

Do we understand what Jesus meant when He said
"…be perfect, as your heavenly Father is perfect"?
Read his entire discourse in Matthew 5, 6, and 7. Then
in your own words explain 5:48 (key word: Therefore).

Consider Jesus…how did He differ from the
perfectionist?

On Being Complete

When we are busy trying to make outward things perfect, what could happen? Matthew 23:23, 27, 28; Revelation 3:2

What can we learn from the following passages?

2 Corinthians 12:9

Hebrews 12:22, 23

James 1:2–4

1 Peter 5:10

On Being Complete

Read Matthew 19:16–22. What was this man depending on? How is this relevant?

Read James 3. In your own words explain verse 2.

What do these passages emphasize? 1 John 2:5; 4:12, 17–19.

According to the following passages, what should be our goal or focus?

2 Corinthians 13:9

Colossians 1:28

Colossians 4:12

Hebrews 13:20, 21

If you have a problem with focusing on the external, trying to make things perfect, try to think back to a possible beginning of your desire to have things that way. Using a separate piece of paper, try to write about it. This is for your own enlightenment but could be shared if you like.

What changes will you need to make to help you overcome an outward focus?

Read Romans 8 and note your thoughts. Again, you don't have to share this unless you want to.

Notes

Lesson 10

"You will NEVER amount to anything."

On Encouraging

On Encouraging

The next "NEVER" statement we will consider is so negative it is demoralizing! Said to a child or teenager it can change the course of their life. "You will NEVER amount to anything" indicates a total lack of acceptance and no hope for the future.

In writing to the Christians in Ephesus, the apostle Paul told fathers not to "provoke your children to wrath." (Ephesians 6:4) Certainly a statement of total discouragement could do that very thing. But are children only discouraged by our words? What about the not so young? Are we no longer in need of encouragement?

Define and compare the following words:

ENCOURAGE

EDIFY

BLESS

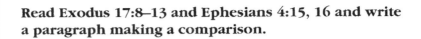

Read Exodus 17:8–13 and Ephesians 4:15, 16 and write a paragraph making a comparison.

In Deuteronomy 1:38 and 3:28 God told Moses to do what? Why? Can you think of how God may be giving us the same instructions?

On Encouraging

In Isaiah 41:1–16 (especially verses 6–10) God
encourages Israel. How does He provide encouragement for spiritual Israel today? See Romans 14:19;
2 Corinthians 10:8; 13:10 Ephesians 4:12

Read the following passages and note some of the
ways that Jesus encouraged others.

Matthew 8:1–3

Matthew 19:13–15

Mark 4:10–15

Mark 14:3–9

John 4:19–26

John 8:3–11

Can you remember the times that Jesus received encouragement from the Father?

On Encouraging

**In the following passages, note who is to encourage
and ways it can be done.**

Romans 14:1–19

Ephesians 6:4; 1 Thessalonians 2:10–12

Philippians 2:1–5

1 Peter 3:1, 2

1 Peter 3:7

1 Peter 3:8

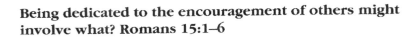

Being dedicated to the encouragement of others might involve what? Romans 15:1–6

No human being is devoid of the need for acceptance and encouragement. It is good for us to go out of our way to build others up, from the young to the elderly. Wouldn't it be great to earn the name given to Joseph of Cyprus in Acts 4:36?

Notes

Lesson 11

"Me submit?... NEVER!"

On Humility

On Humility

What is there about submission that is so threatening? Perhaps one of the problems we have is the idea it is something only women have to do. Actually, women may entertain that idea because it is the way submission is often taught.

The words submit and subject are closely akin to each other. Using a Bible Dictionary or lexicon, write out the definition of each below.

SUBMIT

SUBJECT

On Humility

In the following passages, who is to be in submission (or subjection) to whom?

Romans 8:19, 20

Hebrews 12:9; James 4:7

Ephesians 1:18–23; Philippians 3:20, 21; 1 Peter 3:21, 22

1 Corinthians 15:25–28

Romans 13:1–5; 1 Peter 2:13–15

1 Corinthians 16:15, 16; Hebrews 13:17

1 Peter 5:5

Titus 2:9, 10; 1 Peter 2:18–20

Ephesians 5:21; 1 Peter 2:17; 5:5

On Humility

Ephesians 5:22; Colossians 3:18; Titus 2:5; 1 Peter 3:1, 2

Write a short explanation in your own words of how each of the following verses describes submission.

Matthew 7:12

Luke 9:23

Philippians 2:3–8

1 Peter 3:1–6

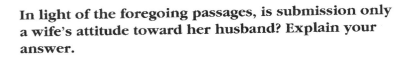

In light of the foregoing passages, is submission only a wife's attitude toward her husband? Explain your answer.

From the following passages note some other characteristics of submission.

Ephesians 4:1–3

Colossians 3:12–14

2 Timothy 2:24, 25

Why do you think submission is so difficult?

Why do you think it is so important for us to have a submissive attitude toward one another?

Is there a time when we should not submit? See Galatians 2:5.

Are there any guidelines for a time like this? Support your answer with scripture.

What should be the goal of our submission?
2 Corinthians 9:12, 13

Notes

Lesson 12

"I could NEVER cope with that."

On Suffering

On Suffering

What are your limits? Perhaps at some time you have said, or heard someone else say, "I could put up with most anything but I could NEVER cope with that!" (The death of my child; the unfaithfulness of my spouse; an alcoholic or drug addicted family member; loss of my home; or a terminal illness. Name your poison.)

How would we respond to tragedy or serious suffering in our life? How can we prepare for an unknown situation of the future? Are there bible examples that can help us? What one man usually comes to mind when we think of tragedy and suffering?

Consider Job's situation and name some of the things that happened to cause him grief. Job chapters 1 and 2

What was the one thing that sustained Job? Job 1:20–22; 6:10; 23:10–12

What was the apostle Paul's attitude regarding his physical suffering? 2 Corinthians 12:7–10

How did Esther deal with a possible calamity? Esther 4

Read Hebrews 4:14–16. How does God relate to our suffering?

On Suffering

What do the following passages tell us about how Jesus prepared for the suffering He knew was ahead of Him?

Matthew 26:36–46

Mark 14:32–42

Luke 22:39–46

John 18:11

find accounts of others who suffered and note how they were able to cope or why they didn't.

What is the main thing we see that enables those who suffer to cope with their trials?

**How can we increase our faith? Romans 10:17;
1 Corinthians 16:13; Ephesians 6:13–19**

**Read the following scriptures and note the outcome of
faith held in times of suffering.**

James 1:3

1 Peter 1:3–9

Jude 20–23

REMEMBER THAT GOD LOVES YOU!
Ephesians 2:4–7; 1 John 3:1

Notes

Lesson 13

Only God can say "NEVER."

On God's Promises

On God's Promises

READ: Hebrews 13:5,6.

You have no doubt heard the saying (or seen the bumper sticker) that says "I don't know what the future holds, but I know who holds the future!" This seems to state pretty well why only God can say "NEVER."

We cannot know what circumstances will occur in the days ahead that can cause us to have a different viewpoint, nor do we know what temptation Satan will hurl in our path or what trial we must bear. We can try to prepare ourselves for various possibilities and fortify our weak spots, but how things will really be will remain unknown until the future becomes the present.

However, it is not that way with our Father in heaven. He has all knowledge. He was able to plan events before the beginning of time, and it can give us a great encouragement to know that the promises He makes will NEVER fail!

How long have people been testing God's promises? Genesis 3:2–6

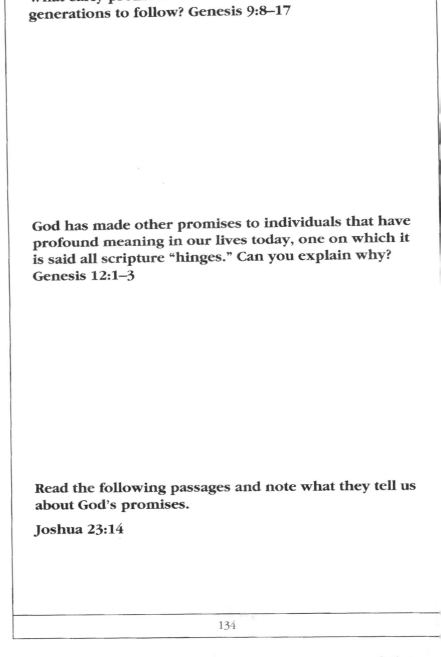

On God's Promises

What early promise was made to one man and all generations to follow? Genesis 9:8–17

God has made other promises to individuals that have profound meaning in our lives today, one on which it is said all scripture "hinges." Can you explain why? Genesis 12:1–3

Read the following passages and note what they tell us about God's promises.

Joshua 23:14

On God's Promises

1 Kings 8:56

Romans 15:8, 9

Hebrews 11:32–34

2 Peter 3:9

What are some things God promises to the faithful?
Matthew 6:25–33

Mark 16:15, 16

2 Peter 1:10, 11

1 John 5:14, 15

Revelation 2:10

On God's Promises

What is promised to the unfaithful?

Psalm 1:6

Mark 16:15, 16

2 Thessalonians 1:6–10

Revelation 20:10

Note what is coupled with the promises in the following:

Deuteronomy 31:6

Psalm 103:17, 18

Matthew 6:33

Mark 16:15, 16

Hebrews 11:32, 33

1 Peter 5:6, 7

**In Romans 15:13 God is called "the God of hope."
Can you explain why?**

**Read the following passages and note how you can be
encouraged by these promises in a personal way.**

John 3:16

John 10:10

Acts 2:38,39

On God's Promises

Hebrews 6:17, 18

James 1:5

1 Peter 1:7–9

1 John 5:4

Knowing that God's promises will not fail, what should our attitude be?

Hebrews 4:16

Hebrews 13:5, 6

1 John 4:17

Do you have a promise passage that is special to you? Share it!

Notes

Notes to the Teacher

Introduction

Although these lessons can be beneficial to someone studying privately, they were designed to be used in classes. The best classes are the ones where those present are willing to take part. The exchange of ideas, experiences, and discoveries during personal study are very valuable. Yet, it is never a good idea to put someone "on the spot" with direct questions unless you are sure they will have a response. The idea of course is to stimulate our thinking...not to elicit "cut and dried" answers.

Encourage everyone to read the lesson you are going to study and have their workbooks filled in so they will be prepared for discussion when class begins. Certainly, you will want to do the same.

When teaching this series you will find there will be more material than can be covered in one hour. You can either allow two weeks per lesson or be selective about which questions you will use for class discussion. Some questions are basic and have obvious answers while others are more challenging. For each lesson, I have tried to summarize to direct you to the personal application we need to make.

Be sure to have a prayer before you begin each class. Prayer, of course, is very important as you study God's word. Please drop me a note, in care of Rockwood Publications, as you begin this series and I will pray for you and your group.

There are some books mentioned for additional reading for those who may need more encouragement in a specific area.

On Commitment

True commitment is complete dedication. A life lived in Christ has no separate compartments, some spiritual and some temporal. All aspects of our lives must be committed to and lived in Him.

We must totally deny our own self focus and surrender to the will of God. This is prescribed by Dr. Luke to be a daily exercise. (Luke 9:23) "Taking up the cross" is a symbol of death...giving over our life completely and willingly as Jesus did ...death of our self will.

Suggested reading: *The Cost of Discipleship* by Dietrich Bonhoeffer.

On Service versus Pride

Read 1 Peter 2:4–9 and think about your concept of what a priest was in God's early dealings with the people of Israel. Someone in fancy robes who burned incense and prayed for the people? A figurehead who was pampered and worshipped?

Now read the first chapter of Leviticus and picture what the priests did when they offered sacrifices. They slaughtered animals and lifted large portions of meat onto the altar, where they had already arranged wood to burn. It was bloody, heavy, hard, smelly work! A work of service.

Peter finally learned that Christians are priests, but not in a position of "holier than thou," rather in a position of service. Jesus as "chief priest" (Hebrews 4:14) was our example and said that He came to serve, not to be served. (Matthew 20:28)

Suggested reading: *The God of the Towel* by Jim McGuiggan.

On Taking a Stand

Isn't it interesting that Jesus said he himself would be the cause of the Apostles "falling away"? Their lack of understanding the purpose of His suffering and death would cause them to desert Him when He needed them most.

Peter's fear and confusion caused him to act like anything but a rock. He shows us it is not enough to follow at a distance or even to "sit in the courtyard." This is halfhearted discipleship and leads to denial.

Our self righteousness says, "I would NEVER do that!" Yet we do in countless little ways. Remember to thank God for His forgiveness, praise Him for His grace, and appreciate His mercy. Then pull yourself up, brush yourself off, and begin again. Peter did!!

On Prejudice

We might try to justify ourselves with our "right" to personal preference, but can we examine its root? Can we admit to ourselves when our preference is based on prejudice?

In spite of any symbolism we might see in the repetition of the vision Peter saw, there is the simple fact that change is hard. We are not born prejudiced; we learn it. Once in place, an unfair dislike resists our effort to remove it.

The gospel of Jesus is for everyone. If we consider others beneath us or inferior in some way, it is very unlikely we will try to share that good news with them.

May God help us truly love one another!

On Teaching

Read the third chapter of James. What is James saying here? "Let not many become teachers" is a caution not to take on the task lightly. There is a great responsibility that goes with it.

Look at the context. While teaching, the things we say (our tongue) can get us into trouble. We can say things that are misleading and that can even cause anger, quarrels and division. "But who is wise and understanding" (verse 13) let him preach? No, "Let him show by his good behavior his deeds in the gentleness of wisdom." This is the most effective way to teach. We must not underestimate it.

Peter said to "be ready always to make a defense to everyone who asks you to give an account for the hope that is in you." (1 Peter 2:15) Why would anyone ask, if our life didn't show them we have hope within us?

Suggested reading: *Out of the Salt Shaker* by Rebecca Manley Pippert.

On Marital Fidelity

It seems to me to be very important to realize that just because you are not vulnerable to a particular sin at one time in your life does not mean you would not be at another. (Galatians 6:1)

Whether David really hadn't recognized his sin or if he was just surprised he had been found out, after going to such great lengths to cover his sin, may be debatable. But whatever the case, the fact remains whether it had remained hidden or not, it was not okay. David had indeed been "moved" from the steadfast path of his God.

Ever heard the old adage "an idle mind is the devil's workshop"? Apparently in his restlessness David allowed unwholesome thoughts into his idle mind. What a dangerous pastime! (Mark 7:20–23) "Our minds feed the fantasy, the fantasy creates the emotion and emotions scream for the actual experience."*

How can we prepare to resist infidelity's temptations?

1. Realize it can happen to you.
2. Discipline your mind.
3. Don't compare your spouse to others.
4. Recognize the differences in men and women. Be aware of what might arouse another.
5. Seek encouragement in the right places.

---

*From *The Myth of the Greener Grass*, J. Allan Petersen © 1983 first edition. © 1991 Revised edition. Used by permission of Tyndale House Publishers, Inc. All rights reserved.

On Forgiveness

Just how important is it to forgive others? Is it necessary to forgive someone over and over again? Of course the answer to both of those questions is, Yes!

Jesus said that when His disciples prayed they should forgive whatever they had against anyone so that the "Father also who is in heaven may forgive you..." (Mark 11:25) An unforgiving heart can block God from forgiving us. Do we consider that when we pray?

What if someone doesn't ask our forgiveness? When viewing the scene at the cross, through gospel accounts, I don't see people begging Jesus for forgiveness. Still, we hear him pray to the Father for that very grace for them. Stephen also showed an example of a forgiving spirit. (Acts 7:59, 60)

When Jesus uses the number seven, in reply to Peter's question of how often he should forgive his brother, He multiplies this symbolic number of completeness to expand the emphasis. What He is saying in essence is...forgive as many times as it takes!

On Parenting

The goals we should want the training of our children to accomplish are:

Respect for God and authority.

Instilling of moral and Godly values.

Fostering of love for God and others.

Healthy sense of self respect and personal responsibility.

There are obviously other ways these goals may be expressed. I have found that in our classes most goals mentioned fit in to one of these categories.

Comparison of Matthew 22:37–40 and Ephesians 6:1– 3:

Children will first learn love at home. The love and respect they learn to show their parents will be a springboard to their attitudes toward those outside their home. "All will be well with them" and they will not disappoint their parents.

We learn "agape" love from God, and our love and respect for Him and His authority are what ignite our loving relationships with others. Our life in Christ will be successful, and we will not disappoint our heavenly Father.

On Being Complete

There are several directions we could take with this subject. I have chosen to focus on the importance of being spiritually mature or complete.

In the "sermon on the mount" (Matthew 5, 6, & 7) Jesus taught what those in His kingdom would be like. Not externally driven, living by the letter of a law, rather living by the spirit of His rule in their hearts. When He said, "Love your enemies and pray for those who persecute you," He knew this would show the true attitude of a child of God, who treats the good and the evil with the same kindness.

Even the wicked love those who love them. How are we different, if we are "perfect," like God, complete with regard to goodness? See an expository dictionary for note on "perfect" in this passage.

Jesus continues (chapter 6) to contrast outward actions and inward attitudes. "Don't practice your righteousness to be noticed." Could this address perfectionism as well as hypocrisy? The same principle continues (chapter 7) and includes anxiety over how things look to others and worry over our daily needs.

Jesus differed from the perfectionist, because He was perfect, but note that He didn't please everyone!

On Encouraging

The writer of the Hebrew letter admonished those early Christians to consider how they could stimulate each other to love and good deeds and not to give up meeting together because they needed that encouragement. (Hebrews 10:23–25)

In comparing Exodus 17:8–13 and Ephesians 4:15, 16, we see a correlation between the way God accomplished His purposes for the Israelites of old and how His people are to carry out His will today, as in the early church. Just as the people needed Moses' encouragement and he in turn depended on the support of Aaron and Hur, Christians now are as dependent upon each other as the members of a physical body. There is just as great a need for supporting and building up as there ever was.

However, if for some reason acceptance and encouragement is lacking from those around us, we can be helped by knowing that the Lord is always there for us and has left His word to encourage us as well.

Suggested reading: *The Blessing* by Smalley & Trent, *Silver Boxes* by Florence Littauer.

On Humility

In our society, a submissive attitude is often thought of in terms like "poor self image" or "character weakness." I personally feel it to be the very opposite of that and feel the Bible bears that out.

In defining words used in this lesson note an important difference. SUBMIT (*hupeiko*) "To yield yourself." SUBJECT (*hupotasso*) "To rank under." One other word is translated SUBJECT (*enochos*) through the fear of death (used in Hebrews 2:15). This is NOT commanded. An attitude of subjection is voluntary but must be attained.

God has shown us love and has given us someone to practice on. (1 John 4:20) It is the same with submission. How can we submit to God, whom we have not seen, unless we learn by practicing submission in our earthly relationships?

On Suffering

Our God can relate to our suffering through the experience of Jesus, who suffered in every aspect while He lived a human life. He experienced trials, temptations, and physical torment. He can be merciful because He knows exactly what we are feeling.

There is also comfort in knowing that nothing can come at us that does not first pass before the throne of God. (Job 1) He has promised us through His word (1 Corinthians 10:13) that He will not allow us to be overtaken by something we are not capable of bearing. He always provides us what we need to endure it. We need to continually confirm our faith and not put up a roadblock to His mercy.

It is also important that we remember our suffering can be a natural consequence of our own sin or bad choices. We must not become bitter and blame God when this happens. Look for the opportunity to grow by it and give God the glory!

Suggested reading: *Where is God When It Hurts?* by Philip Yancey.

On God's Promises

After talking about the things you feel you may or may not be able to cope with in your life, hopefully you have established that faith is the great sustainer. Trust in God and the study of His word is that support that holds us up in tough times.

Obviously we can only depend on someone or something that is stable, unchanging, and constant. The scripture holds forth God as that one. His promises NEVER fail!

Read 2 Peter 3:3–9 and see if we might consider God's promise in Genesis 9:16 as an expression of His patience with mankind.

Really look at the promises of God and see if you don't very often find that they are coupled with an action, stimulated by faith.

> *"Now to Him who is able to do exceeding abundantly beyond all we ask or think, according to the power that works within us, to Him be the glory in the church and in Christ Jesus to all generations forever and ever. Amen."*
>
> —Ephesians 3:20, 21

About the Author

Catherine G. Swift, known as "Geri," teaches Bible classes for women and children and has been well-received as a speaker for women's groups. She and her husband, Jerry, have four grown children and twelve grandchildren. They are active members of a church family in Santa Rosa, California.